Parrot

Series "Fun Facts on Birds for Kids"

Written by Michelle Hawkins

Parrot

Series "Fun Facts on Birds for Kids"

By: Michelle Hawkins

Version 1.1 ~January 2021

Published by Michelle Hawkins at KDP

Parrots do not have vocal cords.

The best way to bond with a Parrot is to give it treats.

Most Parrots are diurnal, active during the day, and sleeping at night, like a human.

Amazon Parrots are the best talking Parrots.

Parrot beaks never stop growing.

Parrots can use their feet to lift their food to their mouth.

Psittacofulvins is a pigment that keeps Parrot feathers their beautiful colors.

Parrots will make the sound they hear to fit in with their environment.

Parrots have feet called Zygodactyl; two toes on the front and two toes on the back.

Scientists think that Parrots have the mind of a four-year-old, so be careful what you say around them.

There are over 350 different types of Parrots in the world.

Parrots can be three inches long to forty inches long.

A Parrot can eat a man's finger if given proper motivation.

Baby Parrots only have down feathers on their back when they are born.

Parrots do not have ears.

Eagle, Hawks, and Snakes are predators of the Parrot.

Parrots enjoy toys that they can chew on, climb on, swing from, or throw them.

In Ancient Times, Parrot feathers were used in decoration for ceremonial purposes.

Parrots can weigh from two ounces up to fifty-six ounces.

Parrots have a strong and curved beak.

Puck, the Parrot, knows over 1,700 unique words.

Steve Irwin feared Parrots but didn't mind snakes.

Baby Parrots do not open their eyes till they are about two weeks old.

Male Parrots woe the female Parrot by dancing, parading, and making unique sounds.

Parrots are found wherever there is a tropical and subtropical region in the world.

A Parrot wingspan can be up to five feet wide.

Parrots eat both meat and vegetables.

Parrots love to be petted, especially on the top of their head.

Parrots mate for life.

Parrots are loud; in captivity, they want to keep track of their owner; they want to keep up with their mate in the wild.

Parrots gather in flocks of up to 100 at a time.

Over one hundred Parrots are on the endangered species list and are facing extinction.

Parrots will taste using the roof of their mouth.

Parrots can dance to rhythmic music.

Parrots are very vocal birds.

Parrots feel emotions like humans do.

Parrots became pets over three thousand years ago.

Parrots need lots of attention; if they become bored with the lack of attention, they could start plucking out their feathers.

Parrots that mate looks very closely alike.

Parrots are known for their upright position.

Parrots can be taught to paint.

Parrots have slender bodies, small necks, and giant heads.

Australia has schools to teach Parrots to talk.

Baby Parrots feather appear at about three weeks of age.

Baby Parrot's feathers are called pinfeathers.

Seeds are Parrots favorite food.

The more colorful the food, the more Parrots like it.

Parrots can live from ten years to up to one hundred years.

Parrots can copy human laughter.

The average heartbeat of a Parrot is 200 beats per minute.

Most Parrots are left-handed.

Parrots enjoy being misted twice a day, which helps with their respiratory function.

The female Parrot will lay between two to eight eggs.

Parrot eggs are white.

Toys and treats help to your Parrot active and not stressed.

Most Parrots sleep at night and are awake during the day.

Parrots can add and subtract.

The Parrot's tongue helps them to eat fruits and seeds.

Parrots have powerful legs.

Mom Parrot will stay with the babies while Dad gets the food for the young and herself.

A group of Parrots is called a Pandemonium.

Most Parrots have blue, green, red, and yellow feathers.

Parrots that are screaming, screeching, and squawking can keep up with the other Parrots in their group.

Parrots can be on the nest for between 17 to 35 days before baby Parrots appear.

In India, it is illegal to keep a Parrot in your home.

Find me on Amazon at:

https://amzn.to/3oqoXoG

and on Facebooks at:

https://bit.ly/3ovFJ5V

Other Books by Michelle Hawkins

Series

Fun Facts on Birds for Kids.

Fun Fact on Fruits and Vegetables

Fun Facts on Small Animals

Printed in Great Britain
by Amazon

83110645R00020